Poems And Verse

Poems And Verse

Illustrations by:
KEITH FURLONG
and
JANET FURLONG

authorHOUSE®

AuthorHouse™
1663 Liberty Drive
Bloomington, IN 47403
www.authorhouse.com
Phone: 1-800-839-8640

Published by AuthorHouse   05/09/2012

ISBN: 978-1-4685-7833-1 (sc)
ISBN: 978-1-4685-7834-8 (e)

Contents

Psalm 104

Praise the Lord, O my soul.
O Lord my God, You are very great;
You are clothed with splendour and majesty.
He wraps Himself in light as with a garment;
He stretches out the Heavens like a tent
and lays the beams of His upper chambers
on their waters.
He makes the clouds His chariot and rides of the
wings of the wind.
He makes winds His messengers,
flames His servants.
He set the earth on its foundations;
it can never be moved.
You covered it with the deep as with a
garment;
the waters stood above the mountains.
But at Your rebuke the waters fled,
at the sound of Your thunder they took to flight;
they flowed over the mountains,
they went down into the valleys,
to the place you assigned for them.
you set a boundary they cannot cross;
never again will they cover the earth.
He makes springs pour water into the ravines;
it flows between the mountains.
They give water to all the beast of the field;
the wild donkeys quench their thirst.
The birds of the air nest by the waters;
they sing among the branches.
He waters the mountains from his upper chambers;
the earth is satisfied by the fruit of His work.

He makes grass grow for the cattle,
and plants for man to cultivate bringing
forth food from the earth:
wine that gladdens the heart of man,
oil to make his face shine,
and bread that sustains his heart.
The trees of the Lord are well watered,
the cedars of Lebanon that he planted.
There the birds make their nests;
the stork has its home in the pine trees.
The high mountains belong to the wild goats;
the crags are a refuge for the wild conies.
The moon marks off the seasons,
and the sun knows when to go down.
You bring darkness, it brings night,
and all the beasts of the forest prowl.
The lions roar for their prey and seek their
food from God.
The sun rises and they steal away;
they return and lie down in their dens.
Then man goes out to his work, to his labour
until evening.
How many are your works O Lord!
in wisdom you made them all;
the earth is full of your creatures.
there is the sea, vast and spacious,
teeming with creatures beyond number living
things both large and small.
There the ships go to and fro,
and the leviathan, which you formed to
frolic there.
These all look to you to give them food at the
proper time.

When you give it to them, they gather it up;
when you open your hand,
they are satisfied with good things.
When you hide your face, they are terrified;
when you take away their breath,
they die and return to the dust.
When you send your spirit, they are created,
and you renew the face of the earth.
May the glory of the Lord endure forever;
may the Lord rejoice in His works He
who looks at the earth and it trembles,
who touches the mountains, and they smoke.

Chapter 1

GOD'S GARDEN

I hope and pray that the poems you are about to read will help you understand that God is our helper in many ways. Life can be for the most an enjoyable experience. God gave us many beautiful things to enjoy in His Creation. He gave us the Trees and flowers and all the wonderful scenery, in many changing colours, to brighten our lives throughout the changing seasons. The first chapter contains a few poems which depict the wonderful garden God created for our enjoyment. As you read these poems, take your mind off worldly cares and feel the comfort and peace of GOD's creation.

Gods Garden

Genesis 1: v,s 1–31
Psalm 1 : vs 3

In that wonderful garden long ago, God created man, to live in peace and harmony with creatures great and small, and God gave Adam a job to do, to give them all a name and God would sit and talk with Him and shelter from the rain. For God created Adam first, so perfect in His sight, and gave Him everything he'd need except of course a wife. Then God in all His wisdom, Adam's loneliness could perceive, so from Adams rib a woman made and God did name her Eve. And in that garden they did live enjoying every day giving names to all the animals and learning how to pray. But then their prayers were different, for they could see our God and walk with Him and talk with Him and know what He had said. But now we have to pray by faith believing that He hears but wishing we could see His face not having any dread. How wonderful it must have been to live with God each day, to sit with Him and talk with Him so let us once more pray.
Dear Father God who made us all and animals so big and small, we pray that one day we will be, in Heaven where we all, will see, you face to face as Adam and Eve, so lets all thank our God in whom we should believe

How Good It Seems

The sun shines bright
the sky is clear,
the day so hot
the air so still,
the silence broken only by the waves
caressing sandy beaches along the shore.
A gull cries out, swooping low
but nothing else invades the peace,
the daily toil a distant memory.
Resting from a time gone by,
alone with God
and thoughts of how things ought to be.
A world at peace,
everyone content to be at one with their Creator.
There but for a moment in time,
how good it seems.

A Glimpse Of Heaven

No matter how you move
or try to re-arrange the plants, the flowers,
trying to improve upon this space,
given but for you and I to share,
as we admire the beauty that surrounds us
in this heavenly place.
For God adorned each plant
and clothed them as to show the world He cares,
and by the very beauty here displayed
reach out and touch,
and feel that here on earth, a glimpse of Heaven,
your heart and mind and soul,
God's peace will inwardly invade.
Surely no where else you'll find a place
no matter how you move, or try to re-arrange,
to suit your mind,
with God's peace and beauty, still remains a place
for you and I to share, a garden here on earth,
a glimpse of Heaven.

Far From Worldly Cares

A garden far from worldly cares
where we can sit in awe of God's creation.
So many flowers nothing can compare,
their beauty no-one can describe,
their fragrance we can only share.
No where else is found that peace,
for inner souls abounds
for you and I to sit in peace,
tranquillity, no-one else to invade our space,
our minds reflecting on God's grace,
for it is He, provider of all this,
and no matter how we re—arrange
the beauty of God's creation still remains,
to hold us here in perfect bliss.
We rest our thoughts and minds
gazing at the colours, shapes, designs
that nothing can compare, or we will find,
outside this garden, far from worldly cares.

God's Colours

God in all His wisdom
made colours mainly green,
so many shades within the world
the like you've never seen.
The sky and sea of blue and white
and clouds of grey and black of night.
In Autumn various shades of red,
the yellows and orange it must be said,
shine forth to brighten the sight we see,
to gladden the heart wherever we'll be,
He did it all for you and me,
what a wonderful God is He.

To Meditate

I sit beneath a willow tree
sheltered from the midday sun,
there's not a cloud that I can see
I sit and meditate alone.
The peace of God is all around
the grass moves gently in the breeze,
butterflies make not a sound
go where they will,
go where they please.
The silence broken by a cry
a magpie makes as he flies by.
The peace of heaven I perceive,
the sky the sun I do receive,
to warm me up and light my day,
to give me rest and let me pray.
I thank you Lord for warmth and light
the sun and moon and stars so bright,
I thank you Lord for all I see,
for beauty, peace, tranquillity,
but most of all for what You've done,
for Jesus Christ, You're only Son,
who brought new life, His light to shine,
for all to see, for all to gain
and like the sun His warmth is given
a radiance of God's true love
that always shines from Heaven above.

As a Rose Protected

The beauty of a rose
so elegantly made,
with overwhelming perfume
your senses to invade,
man tries to re-create
the beauty of this flower
with pot-pourri and scent,
but nothing will empower
or convince me that I'm meant
to understand the reason
such a flower for me was given,
except by God's own hand,
a creation made in Heaven.
The form this flower embodies,
the petals graceful shape
from the bud unto the full grown rose,
no-one can imitate.
From hedgerows and the garden
from walls and trellises,
there hangs the flowers of roses
that no-one can dismiss,
from white and pink and yellow
and crimson velvet to,
such beauty God has given
all meant for me and you.

So stop awhile and marvel
at the rose, but please beware,
for the stems that God gave roses
for protection He made sure,
would spike the hand that tries to steal
this beautiful made flower.
For like us, God gives protection
for everything He's made,
He wants no-one to steal the prize
or to our lives invade,
He sends the holy angels
and like the rose protection given,
to keep us safe and free from harm
until we join Him safe in Heaven.

The Leafy Lane

As I walked along that leafy lane, the trees magnificent in their spring adornment the air was suddenly filled with a heady scent as the hawthorn sprayed its perfume all around.

The blackbird perched high on the chimney singing his happy refrain for all to hear. The sparrows busily darting in and out of the hedgerows tending their newly made nests, chittering and chattering as they go. A couple of collared doves billing and cooing somewhere nearby.

The sun's rays flickering in the branches of the newly adorned beech tree as its branches sway gently back and forth in the warm evening breeze.

The ground is carpeted with pink blossom as it falls gently from the cherry tree.

How good it is to rest awhile and meditate on the perfection of our creative God. To absorb the colours and sounds of peaceful tranquillity

How easy it is to forget the worldly pressures and the stress that man tries to impose upon our lives, trying to suffocate our senses, when surrounded with the soothing balm of Gods creative genius displayed before us.

I praise God for these precious moments, designed specifically for the purpose of our enjoyment, down that leafy lane.

The Peace Of Heaven

The peace of heaven all around,
nothing to disturb my inner calm
all thoughts of earthly pressures drift away.
The sun's rays linger on my face,
so radiant so warm.
The sweet melody of bird song,
like angel choirs, lifting my spirit.
The spring flowers gently bow their heads
in the quiet breeze,
adorned so beautiful, so restful to the eyes.
A garden of Eden such as this,
a gift from God to show us His love.
A place to sit, of peace and tranquillity,
to feel the gentle comfort of God's heavenly kiss.

The Autumn Leaves

The Autumn leaves adorn the trees
so beautiful the colours for us displayed,
the branches gently swaying in the breeze
everything so gracefully arrayed.
The setting sun allows the trees to shine
glorifying God's creative hand,
and all we see is yours and mine
God's wondrous gifts
upon this green and pleasant land.
So spend awhile
reflect upon the sight before your eyes,
magnificent the trees
producing everything we see,
for our surprise.

God's Peace

When all alone, no-one around
nothing moves, there's not a sound,
it's then I feel the breath of God
it's then His presence ever near,
it's then I know He lives in me
to drive away all doubt and fear.
And in the silence I can hear
the Heavenly whispers all around
of angel voices oh so clear.
Then in the presence of the King
my thoughts so plain for all to see,
I know there is no other place,
than here on earth, I'd rather be.
It's here when all alone I stand
with nothing to distract my mind,
in England's green and pleasant land
a quiet corner you will find.
So rest awhile before our God
and listen to the sounds of Heaven,
enjoy the peace that He has given.

In This Place(A Reflection)

What a heavenly place here on earth, sitting quietly,
the wind gently blowing, the sun shining warm in that sheltered
haven of peace.
Leaves moving gently in the breeze, yet glistening,
reflecting rays.
The distant sounds as men toil in the fields,
harvesting GOD's provisions.
Autumn colours almost spent, yet still bringing joy
to our gaze.
Nothing wasted when we stand before a canvas,
painted by GOD's own hand.
So stop awhile, reflect upon GOD's grace.
In this place.

Chapter 2

SHELTER

Again in this section of poems, you are reminded of GOD's creative beauty and also of the perfection in everything He makes. Whilst helping you to relax, in a very hectic and excitable world, God not only provides His birds and animals with protection, He also protects mankind and shows us just how wonderful and thoughtful and perfect are His ways.

Shelter

Examples of GOD's protection:-
Psalm 91 v,s 1-2
Psalm 32 vs 7
1 Corinthians 13: v,s 6-7

Standing tall and proud and silently majestic, providing shelter
and a safe haven for a myriad of God's creatures, hidden beneath
the vast canopy of leafy adornment. The mighty outstretched
boughs supporting the endless branches which in turn support the
glossy mantle of the Summer leaves.

This magnificent tree provides shelter from the rain and stands
firm against the strongest winds and the burning rays of the
midday sun. not many trees can boast so well as this the mighty
oak. Yet as I rest in the shade of the overhanging branches I am
reminded of one whom also stands magnificent above all others
and one who provides shelter and comfort from the storms of life.
Who's mighty outstretched arms enfold us all in the majesty of
His overwhelming love and in whom we can rely on day and
night. And as the mighty oak, our Heavenly Father, our one true
God, stands sure and safe for all eternity.

Stop Awhile

I love to rise at break of day
and watch the sun rise in the sky
and hear the bird song as they
wake and sit and wonder, why?
is man so busy with his life
without the time to even smile,
he struggles with the daily pace
it's about time to stop awhile.
For God created all we see
the beauty of the earth and sky,
He made it all for you and me
so why not live before you die.
Your time on earth may be quite
short, a time that only God can
know,
so stop awhile and let Him show
the reason that He made it all.
A world God formed by His own
hand, with sky and seas and
many lands, God chose the
colours,
blues and greens
and everything for us it seems
we take for granted.
No time to spare,
when all God wants, His love to
share, so before you drive
another mile, before the setting
of the sun,
just thank your God
for all He's done
and stop awhile.

Sit And Rest

We all need time to sit and rest
and take our minds of daily strife,
to meditate upon God's word
and thank the one who gave us life.
For here on earth our time is short
and no-one knows how long we'll live,
except the Holy one above
for life He gave and life He'll take.
Step back, relax, give God a chance
to bring you inner peace and calm,
let Jesus smooth your furrowed brow,
He'll keep you safe and free from harm.
And if you think upon God's word,
be guided by the book of life
and look to Jesus He's the way,
for He will guide you day by day.
So sit and rest your mind and soul
and let God's Spirit set you free,
for He will surely make you whole
and prepare you for Eternity.

The Silence

Listen to the silence, how wonderful and clear,
no noises made by mans own hand
no noises can I hear.
The air is full of peace and calm, serenity assured,
my mind can ponder on God's word
and know that I'm not lured,
into a world of chaos, strife and stress,
that man imposes on your life and yes,
in all the promises he'll make
your peace and happiness he'll take.
So rest awhile and have no fear
the silence bringing God so near,
so listen lest He talks to you
and clear your mind so you can hear,
the whispers that the silence brings
and in your heart God's peace made clear.

The Palm Of His Hand

Nestled there in safety
young birds are warm and safe,
crouched beneath their mother's wings
what more secure a place.
No cares, no fears but for their food
just kept alive by mothers love.
But as they grow and wings mature
it's from the nest that they will fly,
no more to feel that they're secure
no more protected till they die.
But not the same for you and me,
for our protections plain to see
a God who loves and cares for us,
He watches down from heaven above.
If we should fall or feel alone,
if we should cry,
feel hope has gone,
feel no-one cares,
nowhere to turn,
strength ebbed away can't carry on.

Fear not my child for Fathers love
is greater than we understand,
and when we think all hope has gone
He'll take us in His mighty hand,
a place where we are snug and warm,
a place no more to fear or doubt,
a place we really can call home.
For there within that loving palm
the hand of God that reached right in,
the hand that keeps us safe from harm
the hand that keeps us free from sin.
The day we gave our life to God
and we believed in Jesus name
from that day forth and evermore
our lives could never be the same.
And there within that outstretched hand,
protected in that loving palm
He'll keep us till He calls us home.

Gods Protection

Only our Lord could plan in perfect time,
as early days begin to warm,
from lifeless hedgerows suddenly adorned
a profusion of majestic grace appears.
A mantle of white flowers clinging to their sturdy stems,
so tall and proud they stand,
the Hedge parsley, Meadow sweet and Willow herb,
a sight of pure unchartered peace
all produced by Gods eternal plan.
There nestled beneath these gentle giants,
protected by the mantle of the fronds above,
safe from the ravages of stormy days
enveloped and surrounded in the safety of our Gods eternal love.
The faces of the tiny flowers of Lacecap, Speedwell, Buttercup and
Forget-me-not all so colourful and perfect,
a reflection of the intimate relationship between man and God.
We, as they, stand tiny in this endless space,
open to the ravages of life, yet safe,
under the mantle of those eternal arms,
surrounded, protected, sheltered and watched over
by our precious Lord.

The Tree Of Life

A tree stands bare and all alone
empty branches hanging,
no-one seems to care,
and such is life as love for Christ
no-one wants to share.
Yet as the sun warms up the ground
and sap begins to rise,
the tree begins to come to life
before our very eyes,
compare to those who hear God's word
and hearts begin to warm,
and as the bud upon the branch
new life begins to form.
And as the hours and days go by
and buds are opened wide,
those hearts that once were tightly closed
now ask the Lord inside.
For as the leaf clings to the branch
it's life dependant on
and so the hearts of Christians
will cling to Jesus name.
Now as the branches sometimes sway
and leaves fall to the ground,
then so it is with lack of faith
some Christians can be found,
and some will fall and turn away
and others simply leave,
but most will walk the chosen way
and continue to believe.
And as the tree stands tall and strong
adorned in beautiful array,
then this is how God's church must grow
and show the world some-day,
that Jesus is the tree of life
and He's the only way.

In Eternity

How long will take for people to see
that God is the Maker of the sun, moon and sea,
He first made the man to live here on earth
then made him a wife to love and give birth,
to the nations of all time as God has decreed
and from Abraham, Jacob and all other seed,
the sons and the daughters from then until now
with God always leading and showing us how,
to live with each other as His word declares
to love and to care without famine or wars.
Yet as we draw to near to the end of all time
when life as we know it will no longer be,
a new Earth and Heaven God has in mind
where all His believers will eternity see.
So open your eyes and see Jesus, GOD's Son
who will enter your heart when you ask Him to come,
and your personal Saviour He'll always be
and will live with you always in eternity.

Perfector Of Them All

As I breathe the cool night air
reflecting on the day gone by,
my gaze averted for a while
drawn to a picture painted In the sky.
So many stars arrayed so neatly,
forming patterns to guide us on our way,
not there by chance but ordered all in place,
for only God could show us His array
of twinkling perfection in the darkened sky.
And there the brightest of them all
shining magnificent as though to say,
follow me I'll guide you on your way.
We're never lost or all alone
if trusting in His promises the Word has shown,
day or night, the sun, moon or stars so bright,
God is there, perfector of them all.

For Those Who Care

What is life if not for all to share
the pleasant moments,
God gives for those who care
for His creation.
A world He made,
so wondrously displaying
God's creative power,
of land and sea and sky
and mountains soaring high, above,
for all to share and those who care
for trees and meadows
hedges and the like,
the glorious panorama
brought to sight,
for those who care.

The Purity Of Our Lord

God in all His wisdom created everything so good,
all that we survey a reflection of the purity of our Lord.
The colours of the landscape blend together in peaceful serenity,
nothing offensive to our eyes.
The sounds of heaven caress our ears
as the melody of bird song fills the evening air
and the ripple of the stream as the waters wash over the pebbles
on it's way, I know not where.
The rustling of the leaves as a gentle breeze invades their quiet rest,
what glorious wonders to pursue as we gaze upon God's very best.
But there upon a hillside on view for all to see,
man's creation tall and white outstretched arms turning in the wind.
A stark reality, man's invasion upon that quiet calm.
Concrete blocks and high rise flats,
chimneys belching forth their smoke,
the roar of engines, ceaseless noise
as cars and aeroplanes fly by,
must all to God seem quite a joke, as he looks down
from seat on high.
But one day all the noise and clamour
all the sights that hurt our eyes,
all the sounds and everything that man has made,
will disappear and be no more.
For we will see the new creation
God, for us, He holds in store,
no more will man invade God's peace,
no more the noise disturbing rest,
no more offensive sights before us,
churning landscape into dust.
For we will live as one forever guided by His precious word,
in peace, tranquillity and splendour
singing praises to our God.
But whilst we wait for that great moment,
let's focus back on where we are
and view the beauty set before us,
of the purity of our Lord.

Chapter 3

CREATOR OF HUMANITY

In this next chapter I have tried to show how God, as Creator of humanity, wants us to trust Him in everything we do. God is always there to help us and guide us and show us the way forward. He, as our friend, is there to help us thro times of trouble, to guide us when we are uncertain of the path to follow, and to protect us in times of trouble and ultimately lead us to our Eternal home.

Creator Of Humanity

Proverbs 3 vs 5
Psalm 56 vs 4
John 14 vs 1
Colossians 1 vs 15

The air we breathe we cannot see
the wind that blows so strong
and bends the mighty tree,
the sun that shines,
it's heat that shimmers on the tarmac road,
the rain that comes from clouds that dance across the sky
and people that believe that this was made by chance,
I wonder why!
Can they not see the beauty all around
can they not hear the beauty of the sounds,
can they not see that everything was made for you and me?
how can that be?
Was it by chance that rivers formed their course?
was it by chance that mountains first appeared?
was it by chance that we began to breathe?
or is it simply that you can't believe.
Can someone please explain the reason why
that we can laugh and sometimes we can cry?
and sometimes we can sing and sometimes dance,
is this by chance?

There must be something more to life on earth
or why would babies sometimes die at birth?
and why would people suffer needless pain
if there was nothing more on earth, for us to gain?
Why is it that we choose to close our eyes
why is it that we cannot recognise?
that this is just a glimpse of things to come
if we would just believe in God's own Son,
and all the beauty displayed for us to see
is just a glimpse of God's eternity?
It's not by chance that you are here
but by the hand of God,
and was on the cross of Calvary
that God chose to shed His blood.
When Jesus died and rose again
He set us free from sin and pain,
that one day we would all be free
to live for all eternity.
Enjoy your life whilst here on earth
and all the beauty that we see,
and please believe in Jesus Christ
Creator of humanity.

Lonely Bethel

Set apart for all who care to come,
this lonely bethel, but a faithful few call home
and worship God as only they know how,
yet, never doubting, one day all will venture in.
For Just as sure as night time follows day
and with the passing of each encroaching hour,
Jesus will beckon to show them all the way
to save their souls from sinking even lower.
So view this place, empty save a faithful few,
who pray the day will surely come
when people moved by Spirit power
will want to enter in
and fill their hearts with God's pure love
and born again, renewed in their belief,
that Jesus lives, forgiving all their sins.
So lonely bethel set apart,
waiting for that glorious day,
when God will call them all to pray
and sing their praises to our Lord,
and thank Him that within His word,
for those that truly do believe,
Eternal life they will receive.

Put Your Trust In Me (Matt.8)

The storm it raged, the waves were high,
the boat was tossed and thrown about,
and Jesus lay there in the stern,
fast asleep, there is no doubt.
The disciples they were sore afraid
the sea would drown them all,
there was only one thing they could do,
on Jesus they would call.
Master, Master please wake up,
we're all about to die,
so Jesus stood and calmed the sea
and then He did reply.
All of you of little faith,
you men who've walked with Me,
and seen the miracles I've performed,
I've even calmed the sea,
now knowing that I've kept you safe,
in future put your trust in Me.

Miracles

Jesus made the lame to walk,
the deaf to hear, the blind to see,
He even raised the dead to life
and calmed a raging sea.
Yet even though He did all this
they nailed Him to a cross,
and mocked and jeered and spat at Him
until our dear Lord died,
and everyone that loved Him so
and even angels cried.
Yet Jesus rose again to life
and by His Spirit gives,
a new life born in all of us
but first we must believe.
And all the miracles Jesus did
He said that we can do
you only have to show, by faith,
He lives inside of you.
For nothing is impossible
when Jesus lives within
and by His Holy Spirit
healing will begin.
So claim the words that Jesus gave
and do the works He did,
believing only in His word
and promises He made.

Can We Trust In God

When you put your trust in God
He will not fail you or deceive,
for God has written in His word
that in His Son if you believe,
a home for all eternity awaits
for all who ask Him in,
when on your door He knocks and waits,
to welcome you to Heaven's gates.
And since your life on earth began
and God bestowed His love on man,
reward for faithfulness He gives
and all good things will you receive,
and every life He wants to save
and in His Son if you believe,
Eternal life, a Heavenly home
to share with all who trust our Lord.

All That I Am

The Lord is my guide in all that I am
there's nothing that He won't provide,
giving me peace and the quiet and calm
He's constantly there by my side.
My mind and my soul
restored by His will
in righteousness leading me on,
His namesake guiding me still.
In days that are dark
and where battles rage on
I fear not the arrows that fly,
for there by my side
You will stay and will guide
and will comfort me all of the way.
To mine enemies shown a victory won
my head is anointed with oil
and the joy I receive of pure goodness and love
will remain for the rest of my days,
until I am called home to the glories above
and with my Lord for eternity stay.

How Blest Am I

How blest am I that you chose me
to set apart in this place of beauty and tranquillity,
to rest my mind from the weariness of daily strife
to set before me a cascade of sheer delight,
encountering the pleasures You have given me to view,
whilst my body soul and spirit commune as one with You.
Reflecting on the past and grieving for a moment
on pleasures lost but instantly refreshed,
reminded of a hope we have in You,
kissed by a gentle breeze as though caressed by the breath of an angel,
surrounded by hope,
how blest am I.
Amazed I stand and listen to His voice, so clear,
in the rustling of the leaves,
choirs of angels transported on the breeze,
I catch a glimpse of Heaven
oh what more can I perceive,
how blest am I.

ℐ 𝒦𝓃𝑜𝓌

I know there's a God and I know that He's real,
how do I know?
By the way that I feel,
for the ways that He helps me each day of my life
and guides and protects me in trouble and strife,
for the hope that He's given to you and to me
and the way we're forgiven, for He hung on a tree.
His life He surrendered and all sins He did bear
and in His resurrection a new life He did show,
and all that He asks is that we truly believe,
accepting forgiveness and freely receive
all that He gives us, His kindness and love,
free gifts from the Father, free gifts from above.
I know I'm not worthy to look on His face,
but I'm saved for Heaven, I'm saved by His grace,
I'm saved for a kingdom and will for eternity live
with my Father in heaven and all angels above
and all gone before me and all those I love,
and all that He asks is we freely speak out,
the name of our Saviour, the name of our Lord,
to be witnesses for Him and believe in His word.
I know there's a God, if it were not so,
my life would have ended a long time ago.
We all have our troubles and burdens to bear,
but life is made easier, when with Jesus we share.
So join with me now in praising our Lord
and praying for those who don't know of His word,
for I know that one day, when this life is done,
and God calls us home, I'll know that we've won
and we'll live forever with Father, Spirit and Son.

No-One knows

No-one knows the will of God
or understands how it should be,
for only He, Creator of it all
the one who gave us life
to live in harmony, with Heaven's created beings,
our guardians formed to guide our paths
and protect us on our way.
No-one knows the hour when He will come again
and draw us to our Eternal home,
His word is clear to watch and be prepared,
for one will go and one be left alone.
So prepare your hearts and make ready for the call,
accepting God as Saviour of mankind,
who rose from death and there by grace you'll find
that where there once was darkness now there's light,
and understanding of His word and clarity of mind.
No-one knows tomorrow for we live within this day,
yet staying ever faithful and walking in GOD's way,
and keep your hearts and minds on Him,
stay focussed on His Son,
sing praises to our Saviour
and when He claims His own,
it's then we'll know the will of God
with understanding given,
who prepared for us Eternal life
to live with Him in Heaven.

Open

Open your eyes and see,
the glory of our risen Lord.
Open your ears and hear
the message from the written word.
Open your heart and feel,
the Spirit of God, who'll enter in.
Open your mind and know,
that your life has just begun again.

I Never Knew

I never knew that born again meant asking Jesus in.
I never knew that Jesus died to take away my sin.
I never knew He did it all so that we could be with Him.
I never knew He rose again to live with God in Heaven.
I never knew that I could feel so different deep inside.
I never knew that all my thoughts from God I cannot hide.
I never knew that from that day how different I would be.
I never knew that I'd been blind but now I really see.
I never knew that in my heart Jesus would remain,
and since that day I asked Him in,
I've never felt the same.

Chapter 4

LOVE

This final chapter, entitled Love, shows just how much God loves His children (us) in that He sacrificed His only Son for you and me. The ultimate sacrifice in any family, would be to sacrifice your own life so that your children might live. God sacrificed His Son so that we all might live. These poems show you that without love you have nothing. God teaches us how to love one another, just as Jesus loved, and indeed still loves us. I pray that as you read these final poems, you will appreciate the way in which God teaches us how to love. May God bless you all as you read these poems and the scriptures attached to them.

Bond Of Love

John 3 :16
John 15: 9–10
1 Corinthians 13 : 4–13
Ephesians 5: 1–2

Father in Heaven, grant to us that we may be a reflection of Your perfect love. That in our weak moments when our thoughts are blurred by worldly pressures and realities seem so hard to overcome, remind us that all things are possible, that our hopes, dreams and aspirations are made reality, when we take our eyes off the world and focus them on you.

You created us, brought us together and joined us as one to be a channel of your peace. Because of our transgressions, we turn the calm sea into troubled waters, the gentle breeze into a strong wind and the light rain into a torrential downpour. when all seems lost and our lives in danger of being washed away on a tide of hopelessness, confusion and despair, Jesus will once again stand up and speak to the troubled waters and calm the angry sea.

As we remember that Jesus is the way, the truth and the life, then one day soon, I am convinced that we all will walk together along the shore of that calm sea, where all our troubles will fade into a distant memory and we will all walk together in a bond of unified love as God intended.

Amen.

God Is Love

There are no preconditions
set by God or by His Son,
for they have loved us all
since the day that we were born,
and nothing you or I can do
will change the way They feel,
for loving us the way They do
is very, very real.
For sinners more than anyone
are saved by God's pure grace,
not by being righteous
will you earn a place,
with God, His Son and everyone
who believe in Jesus name.
For when God sacrificed His Son,
He looked down from Heaven above,
He did it all for you and me
to show the world,
that God is love.

Love

One day death will take life from the ones that we love,
so whilst you live, make sure you love life,
for life is given from God up above
and through God we receive the ability to love.
God, in His wisdom, gives freely His love,
so remember to share this gift that He shows.
Then one day you'll see Jesus and He'll tell you He knows,
all the love that He gave you, to others you showed,
for love truly is given, a gift from above,
a gift to give others, a gift we call love.

Made Perfect

A baby cried as new birth appeared
that tiny form made perfect,
held in its mothers arms
the bond of love made clear.
And so it was with Mary
who held our Saviour close to her
the birth as natural as any other,
the child made perfect in the sight of God
yet conceived by Spirit, to a chosen mother.
And as the child did grow
as to the form of man,
yet only in appearance
for since the world began,
the Son of God would come to earth
and as a baby grow,
into the Saviour of mankind
so everyone would know,
that God thro His Eternal plan
gives everyone the chance
to give their hearts and lives to Him,
our God that came as man.
That tiny child that Mary bore,
conceived by God's pure Spirit,
who lived and died to save the world,
the Son of God made perfect.

With Grateful Heart

With grateful heart I thank you Lord
for once again upon this day,
you've surely proved your love for me
and guided me upon life's way.
With grateful heart I praise Your name
for I just know You're by my side,
and I will never be the same
knowing You will be my guide.
With grateful heart I have no doubt
that in this world so full of sin,
all can be saved by Jesus name
unlock the door and let Him in.
With grateful heart I'll do my best
to take your word to all I can,
and teach them of our gracious Lord
and how they can be born again.
With grateful heart I kneel and pray
and thank my God for saving me,
and I'll go forward in His way
and live for all eternity.

I Praise My Lord

The sky is dark and bears an angry face,
the clouds driven like sails before the wind,
my body shivers in the cool refreshing air
as it rushes on its way, I know not where,
the warm sun of yesterday hidden from sight
and yet I know that it's still there.
The birds hidden in the trees,
sing melodious songs sheltered by the leaves.
I stop, a while, to gaze across to distant hills
and as I rest my mind,
the sun appears, glinting on the meadow laid before me,
the tall grass happy to be bathed in the warmth of its rays
as it stands proud before the stiffening breeze.
No matter how strong the wind may blow
or dark and angry the sky appears,
no matter how battered and bent the tall grass seems,
the sun still shines and all our fears,
are borne away on the gentleness of GOD's embrace.
I praise my Lord for showing me,
that in the darkness of the skies
and the turmoil of our lives,
GOD's always there and will always be,
to show His love for you and me, reminding us to never fear,
nor doubt His word,
but trusting in our Saviour and our precious Lord.

A Friend Like Mine

Do you want a friend like mine
who never leaves you night or day,
who always loves you
never judges what you say,
never argues always fair
never angry always there,
to help you in your time of need
to hold you when you're tired and sad,
to listen when you start to plead
make you happy, make you glad.
Do you want a friend like mine
who died that you might live again,
who suffered anguish, suffered pain,
bore the sins of all mankind.
And at the door He knocks and waits
and in your heart I think you'll find
that Jesus is that friend of mine,
hoping you will let Him in
to welcome you to Heaven's gates.

For All Believers

Oh such love that God has shown to all Mankind
especially those who chose His Son,
and in whose name believes in everlasting life
not here on earth but for a time made perfect
for all to share.
As we go forth and live each day
guided by the hand of God and living in His word,
we speak to God thro Jesus His own Son
who won for us a victory and in the gap now stands
to intercede on our behalf,
and on the day we come before the throne of grace,
where all around,
surrounded by the glories of that Heavenly place,
Our Lord and Master, Father God and
Holy Spirit of the Word,
we will meet them all and standing face to face,
will claim the prize for our enduring faith,
and there for all eternity will reign, in perfect harmony,
with all the saints and sinners gone before,
forgiven by the love of God,
and for all believers of the risen Saviour,
Jesus Christ our Lord.

Eternal Home

Lord Jesus help me if you can
help me be a better man,
change my life so I can be
a better follower of Thee.
Each day I walk my life on earth
give it meaning, give it worth,
let me give a helping hand
help me Lord to understand.
Give me wisdom when unsure
of an answer I should give,
to how our daily lives we're leading
how our lives on earth we live.
Help me trust You more dearly
walking closer day by day,
following your word more clearly
teaching me in every way.
I know one day I'll stand before You
I pray I'm worthy of Your throne,
and I'm accepted as I am Lord
to enter my Eternal home.
Amen.

Psalm 104 vs. 33-35

33 I will sing to the Lord all my life;
I will sing praise to my God as long
as I live.

34 May my meditation be pleasing to
Him, as I rejoice in the Lord.

35 but may sinners vanish from the earth
and the wicked be no more.
Praise the Lord, O my soul.
Praise the Lord.
Selah